A Century of Poems

To commemorate the 100th Anniversary of VGH Nurses Alumni

Compiled by Madeleine McNeil

A Century of Poems
Copyright ©2020 Madeline McNeil

ISBN: 978-1-927529-90-4
MacKenzie Publishing
Halifax, Nova Scotia
April 2020

Front cover images:
White Point Beach - Painting by Mary Sue MacKenzie, Class '61B
Homecoming 2020 Logo - Designed by Gloria Stephens, Class '53A

Back cover:
Victoria General Hospital - photo by John Ashcroft

All Rights Reserved.

No portion of this publication may be reproduced, stored in any electronic system, or transmitted in any form or by any means, electronic, mechanical, photocopy, recording, or otherwise without written permission from the author.

ಸಿಂಜ
MacKenzie Publishing

Acknowledgements

Time and unknown make it impossible to thank the many who contributed to this collection, but to those whose original vision it was to write your thoughts in verse and leave in print for future generations to read and enjoy, thank you.

Madeleine McNeil
March 2020

Artist's Description of Painting of White Point

I do trust my 61B classmates but they did let me down once, the day I agreed to do a painting of White Point Beach.

We moved back to Halifax in 2000, after being away for years. I was thrilled to be part of the planning committee for the next reunion and travelled with a small group to have a look at the chosen site. Someone suggested we all do a craft for the gift bag as it would be more personal, less expensive and fun.

Guess what? I painted White Point Beach with limited paints and less talent. No one else made a craft.

I used the painting to make laminated bookmarks for everyone. It was the only craft in the gift bag that year. Often wonder if any were used, maybe some are still out there. I still trust my classmates though, completely.

Mary Sue MacKenzie
Class '61B

Foreword

It was during one of our many drives together, on the way across the Angus L. McDonald Bridge, to an Alumni meeting, that Madeleine casually mentioned she had put together "some poems". Over time, she had found them in the VGH Nurses Archives among years of newsletters and archival materials. She wondered if it would be something of interest to Alumni attending the Homecoming in 2020.

Many of us know of Madeleine's dedication to all things Alumni. For many, she is the only treasurer we've known! She has served in that capacity since 1999. Her commitment to keeping the books while at the same time keeping track of membership has been remarkable. It can be said she is a big part of the glue that has kept the Association moving forward.

What many may not know about Madeleine is the time and effort she has given to preserve the VGH Nurses Archives. To facilitate this work, she attended workshops and training programs at the Council of Nova Scotia Archives. In this endeavour, she received the prestigious Dr. Phyllis Blakely Award on behalf of the VGH Nurses Archives for archival excellence. In 2011, she also received the Anna Hamilton Award established in 2004 to honour one volunteer each year who has served the Nova Scotia archival community with sincere dedication.

Her numerous professional credentials include organizing policies and procedures for the newly built Scarborough Centenary Hospital in 1967. She staffed the Medical/Surgical Intensive Care Unit and Post Op Recovery Unit, and then established the Coronary Care Unit until returning to VGH in 1972. In February 1974, she equipped and staffed the first Cardiovascular Care Unit there.

Her many accomplishments were recognized during the 100th Anniversary of the College of Registered Nurses of Nova

Scotia, when she was the recipient of a Centennial Award of Distinction.

Much has been written about the Art of Nursing but seldom seen is a book of poetry on the subject.

This collection was gathered from a number of archival sources by VGH Nurses Alumni Member Madeleine McNeil to commemorate the 100th Anniversary in 2020. It gives us glimpses from a variety of personal experiences throughout the span of a century: students learning the art, graduates honing their skills, and patients receiving care, along with comments from a variety of observers of the art.

This is a unique and lasting tribute to nursing from the voices of those it has touched.

Joyce (Stevens) Baxter
February 2020

Contents

WRITTEN BY VGH STUDENTS AND GRADUATES 1

When I Have Time – VG Grad, Name Unknown, Class '20.......3
A Leisurely Trip Down Memory Lane – Class '41 4
Days in the Main O.R. – Virginia (Rice) Wile, Class '41 7
Private Hall – Thelma Potter, Class '42 9
Haz's Jammies – Joan Whalley, Class '51B................................10
Thoughts – Edith Anne Gillis, Class '52B 11
The Vague Specific – Edith Anne Gillis, Class '52B.................13
Blessed Are They – Fran C. Fraser, Class '52B 15
The Night Nurse – Miriam Pulsifer, Class '52B 16
Undergraduate Students – Yvonne Myler, Class Feb. '53 17
An "If" for Grace Affiliates – Audrey Young,
   Class Sept. '54 18
Grace Affiliation – Cecilia Powell...20
H.C.H. Affiliation – Betty (unknown).......................................21
Famous Last Words of the Class of Sept. '55 23
Songs of Our Times – Class Sept. '55 24
We'll Never Forget – Class Sept. '55 25
Can You Imagine – Class Sept. '55 26
Ode to "Our Class" – Barbara Miller & Jean Harris,
   Class Sept. '55 27
To Us Seniors – Myrtle Rogers, Class Sept. '55 28
Neurosurgery Night Duty – Myrtle Rogers,
   Class Sept. '55 30
Us – Eleanor Graham & Joan Gregson, Class Feb. '55.............32
Days Spent in the Nurses Infirmary – Dot Creelman,
   Class '55B..34
What Nursing is to Me – Betty Ann Ross, Class '55B..............36
Motherly Advice – Betty Ann Ross, Class '55B........................37
Our Magic Work – Betty Ann Ross, Class '55B........................38
1st Day O.R. – Rosemarie Masey, Class '56B............................39
To the Students at the VGH – Carole Reynolds,
   Class '58A..41
40th Reunion VGH Class '61A, Barrington,
   June 2001 – Pat Perry, Class '61A 42

45th Reunion '61A – Pat Perry, Class '61A 44
A Question of Belief – Gail Warren, Class '61B 46
A Tribute to '61B for 55th Reunion, August 2016,
   Joyce (Stevens) Baxter, Class '61B 47
A Nurse's Prayer – Ruth Winant Wheeler 49
It All Began in '63 – Sue (Campbell) Carter, Marg
   (Grandy) Hibbert, Joanne (Dennison) McCormick, Jude
   (Shakespeare) Bell, Class '66A 50
Untitled Memories – Susan (Campbell) Carter, Class '66A..... 51
A Glimpse Inside – Marjorie Pringle, Class '72A 53
Nurse of the Future – Kim Ward, Class '80 55
Of Your Color or Race You Have No Choice, Class '81 56
It's Up to You – Lloyd Ira Miller 57
Leavin' the Old An' Greetin' the New – Lawrence
   Hawthorne 58
Let's Keep in Touch – Virginia Swan 59
Graduation Night – Della May Scott, Class '47 60
Ode to VGH Nurses Alumni 1920-2020 – Joyce (Stevens)
   Baxter, Class '61B 61

WRITTEN TO THE MUSIC OF POPULAR TUNES 63

To the tune of "Land of Hope & Glory" – Probie Song.
   Class '53A.. 65
To the tune of "The Glow Worm" – Probie Song,
   Class Sept. '56... 66
To the tune of "Roll Out the Barrel" – Probie Song,
   Class '61B 67
To the tune of "Mem'ries" for the 50th reunion 2011 –
   Joyce (Stevens) Baxter, Class '61B 68

WRITTEN BY AUTHORS UNKNOWN 69

The Bedpan 71
Ode to a Johnny Shirt.. 72
The Nurses Cap 73
Nurse Defined 74
God Made a Nurse 75

A Nurse's Prayer of Compassion 76
Nurse's Prayer 77
A Nurse's Prayer 78
Just a Nurse 79
Ten Commandments for Probies 80
A Show to Remind Us 81
Thoughts of a Graduate 82
Operating Room Psalm 83
Class Prophecy 1939 84
Life's Changed, Ain't It! 87
To My Mother/To My Father 89
And a Song to Make a Laugh 91
Question in Anatomy 92
Motto for X-Ray 93
My Roommate 94
Needles 95
A Nurse Has Feelings Too 96
Today…Tomorrow…Always 98
Thoughts at 3 a.m. 100
Graduation Teardrops 102
Graduation Song 103

WRITTEN BY PATIENTS AND OTHERS 105

The Nurse – Myrtle K. Wentzell, Patient at VGH, 1940 107
Kindness Heals – James E. McManus, Patient on
   4th Floor 108
Tribute to the Night Nurse – Unnamed ex-patient 109
Oh, Florence Be Glad That You're Dead – Bunny Lord,
   St. Boniface 110
Playing Patient – Edgar A. Guest 112
The Nurse – Edgar A. Guest 113
Farewell 114

**Written by VGH Students
and Graduates**

When I Have Time

When I have time my only thought will be
To make life happier and more free
For those whose lives are crowded now with care
I'll help to lift them from their low despair
When I have time!

When I have time the friend I love so well
Shall know no more those weary toiling
I'll lead her feet in pleasant paths always
And cheer her heart with words of sweetest praise
When I have time!

When you have time; the friend you held so dear
May be beyond the reach of all your sweet intent
May never know that you so kindly meant
To fill her life with sweet content
When you have time!

Now's the time! Oh! Friend no longer wait
To scatter loving smiles and words of cheer
To those around whose lives are now so dear
They may not need you in the coming year
NOW IS THE TIME!

VG Grad, Name Unknown, Class '20
Found among items housed in the Archives

A Leisurely Trip Down Memory Lane

This is a little trip down memory lane
It brings moments of laughter and twinges of pain.
We graduated in '41, 53 years ago
To make it to 55 we have two more to go.

In 1938 we came to the V.G., we were young, smart
Beautiful and good, in '94 we are still good.
There was much in between to take away youth
While we were still searching for honour and truth.

Our probie blue gowns we wore with such joy
You missed out on that Don, too bad you're a boy.
Every morning at 6 when Kit rang the bell
Oh how we wished that she would sleep in.

The hub of our universe was the T.S.O.[1]
When you got a call you had to go
Use common sense lectured Miss Strum loud and clear
This we remembered year after year.
Sick people are not normal, Miss Strum did say
This was soon proved day after day.
When the black stockings and shoes marched down the hall
That was an omen, a bad day for all.
We ran to wash the bedpans and rushed behind screens
Anywhere, anywhere so as not to be seen.

We think of the wards as months of night duty
Under Miss Young we sure lost our beauty
Night duty was 12 hours, oh when did we eat?
Just to keep moving was remarkable feat.

Midnight lunches could have been so good
We had lots of water but so short of food
However, from home would come boxes of food
And barrels of apples, it all tasted so good.

---

[1] Training School Office

We had many lectures which we all slept through
By Miss Joncas and Miss Page to mention a few.
Then to the diet kitchen to cook and to bake

But our best efforts caused Miss Holder to quake.
This is a dry garbage and this is the wet
These were instructions we could never forget.

Then came the O.R., it sure was like hell
Unless you liked blood and gore then it was swell.
O.R. in the pavilion with Powers was great
But in the main with Goss you soon met your fate.

Private Hall had us all at one time or another
And we all had a cry there and wished for our mother.

Of course there was isolation, some bumps or a rash
And you'd break the record for the 100 yard dash.
We were on our own there and just kept things humming
But always a lookout in case Pagie was coming

Fashions by Chittic, she was our haute couture
These were the days before St. Laurent and Dior
The pockets were great but when filled to the top
With eggs, bread and milk cause a most peculiar walk.

We all went to the Grace except Donny C.
What an experience how lucky was he.
Night duty at the Grace, nursery nurses made dinner
A very good reason why we all got much thinner.
The babies were sweet, the mothers just so so.
We had them ten days, then they had to go.
Ginny sang Brahms Lullaby in a voice sweet and clear
We hoped it would reach some howling babe's ear.
Our late leave pass could be a double
If Flick was on duty there would be no trouble

Then came the black band, it took three long years
Of hard work and laughter and also some tears
But hard work and happy times blended together
Made for friendships that have lasted forever.

In 1938 we came to the V.G. we were young, smart,
Beautiful and good, in 1994 we are still good.

Don C. has retired but he keeps going still
We cannot keep up with him, we are over the hill
Does he use Energizers – could we ask?
Because our up and go just does not last
While he keeps going on and on, on and on, and…

Class '41

Days in the Main O.R.

Every new nurse dreads the G.Y.N.
She's down there alone with a couple of men
When Atlee starts swearing, it isn't so cheery
But when he's all through he says "O.K. Dearie"

You walk into "B" to meet your doom
For Dr. Colwell is in charge of the room
He's like a bear when he gets sore
And he throws all the instruments on the floor

He's not so bad if he doesn't have to wait
But he goes to work at an awful rate
When he's all finished there's thankfulness
And he leaves the room in one H--- of a mess

Then there is Eddie Ross and Dr. Currie
They never do things in much of a hurry
As long as you have everything that they need
All is O.K. and everyone is pleased

Now Dr. Goss is the great "I am"
He's a very good surgeon and he does all he can
He takes his time and he ploughs right through
And when he's all finished – the nurses are too.

But when Dr. Kinley enters the room
Instruments fly and things start to boom
By the time the nurse turns around for the cup
He's all finished and "sewing her up"

Then comes Mader and old H.K.
Everybody's quiet and out of the way
He breaks all the needles when he starts to suture
And you wish to the Lord, he was off in the future.

Dr. Mack is the water works man
He looks at the tongue and decides that he can
Make everything run and work like new
With the help of a catheter, a bottle or two.

Now Dr. Schwartz is a remarkable man
He never can think and no one else can.
"Bring me the thing, Nurse", is all he can say
By the time you bring it, it's "take it away".

And so you go on from one to the other,
The girls often wish they were home with their mother.
It's an interesting life, if ever there was one
But you work and you worry like a son-of-a-gun.

Virginia (Rice) Wile, Class '41

Private Hall

Here we are, all snug and fine, in our beds of white.
Hoping to get out again as soon as we're alright.
We like the rest, we like the sleep, we like the service too,
But, oh dear me! It's hard to be content and not get blue.

There's Parker, just across the hall,
she reads and reads and reads,
Jokes, fictions, truth and all, against professional creeds.
Her nose has bothered her today, she had it x-rayed thrice,
And then 'twas packed with cotton wool,
It certainly wasn't nice.

These antrums, they're a nuisance, they cause a lot of pain,
And Dr. Doull does his best to honour the Doull name.
There's Ives next door, a "cold" she has,
her temp one hundred one.
She'll no doubt be here days and days,
till finally it goes down.

And Galleyhew came in today with pain and ache and chills.
Dr. Lehv has visited her, a hot water bottle for her ills.
So life goes on in Private Hall, we all agree we hate it.
But it's the place to get the rest, so that we all can take it.

Thelma Potter, Class '42

Haz's Jammies

An apparition does appear,
Second floor west if you'd care
To see a strange but thrilling sight
Haz – all decked out for the night.

(Her Mother took her at her word
"How fat she's getting is absurd"
And so sweetly did she send
Jammies, that would really tend
To make one think of 44,
Or perhaps, one size more.)

These flannel jammies of blue and white
Most certainly are not too tight
In fact, they follow Haz around,
And trail a little on the ground.

The jacket – newest fashion note
Billows about like a shortie coat,
It's finger-tip and Peter Pan,
Enough to capture any man!

Post Script:
Haz is going down to scrub
She throws those jammies in the tub
The water's hot – a little bit,
And now – those jammies really fit!

Joan Whalley, Class '51B

Thoughts

Of a Probationer…
To be a nurse was my desire,
That's all I'd ever ask –
But since I entered a month ago,
I've found it an awful task.
So many subjects I have to study
And so many things to learn –
I sit and wonder if the time will come
When my cap and bib I'll earn.

Of a Junior…
Ah! Now I'm capped and bibbed like the rest,
I feel like somebody new.
The first year's the hardest, I keep telling myself
And wondering if it is true.
But I've gotten this far and on I'll go –
(My feet feel like they're roasted)
Now all I've got to worry about
Is when my first night duty's posted.

Of an Intermediate…
Well! I can breathe another sigh of relief:
Night duty's not bad after all.
I can see the light ahead of me now,
And vacation's just next fall.
I'm thinking lots different than a year ago,
And in "whites" I'll walk so breezy:
Big trees from little acorns grow,
All things are hard before they are easy.

Of a Senior…
That big oak tree, I've found didn't grow
From an acorn with no ambition:
Energy and persistence conquer all things,
Let them stagnate under no condition.
If one weary soul I have succeeded to ease,

When each day's work is done
I'll know no joy that lies deep as peace,
No peace so deep as that by struggle won.

Of a Graduate…
I realize now since I've reached the top,
I can't just drift to and fro:
More education lies at my feet,
There is so much more to know.
Humanity cries for our services meagre,
In any field we seek –
God's Righteous hand is our reward…
Only there shall we reach the peak.

Edith Anne Gillis, Class '52B

The Vague Specific

What's with seniors and charge nurses
Who point their finger at me:
"How's Jiggeroo? Where's Whozeybug?
Did Whatzit get his tea?
When's 21 due to go?"
(To the O.R. I gather)
"Did 'the heart' in the ward
Get his pill at noon?
And how's 'the leg' down the corridor?
Did Dr. Jigger see "What's hername?
Did he write her prescription too?
The compresses aren't on,
Penicillin's to give:"
(Spilled ink, I'm not white, I'm blue)
"Tell the other nurse she's off duty",
(There's only three it might be
And 4 o'clock is such a long time,
I'm wishing it were me)
"Check the treatment book,
And the blue sheets carefully,
And give Mrs. Jones her stuff.
Mrs. Smith wants a pill,
What kind does she get?
Says it's never enough.
Dr. Doings was in to see Jigger,
The O.R. just called the 'spleen'
And X-Ray wants the 'fractured hip':
You know the one I mean.
Mrs. Whatchacallum needs water,
Mr. Bingo needs a shave.
There's treatment to give Mrs. You know who,
And 56 is for Cardio-Wave."

Why can't calmness take the place of confusion?
Medical terms and Christian names prevail?
'Cause if I give Jigger, Whozeybug's pills,
All these months I've spent will be of no avail!

Edith Anne Gillis, Class '52B

Blessed Are They

Blessed are the students who have just entered training:
For theirs is a noble profession.

Blessed are they who have earned their caps:
For they have climbed the hardest step.

Blessed are those nurses who are patient and understanding:
For respect and love will be theirs.

Blessed are our supervisors who have been our guides:
May our success be their reward.

Blessed are they who have left our fold:
For they will not be forgotten.

Blessed are the doctors for their teaching and reassurance:
To them we give our thanks.

Blessed is He who has watched over us these last three years:
And has given us the courage to go on.

Blessed are our classmates for their loyal friendships:
May these friendships never end.

Fran C. Fraser, Class '52B

The Night Nurse

Corridors hushed and dimly lit,
Voices mute, day noises still:
'Tis a hospital at night,
Where the night nurse guards the ill.

Through the stillness comes a call:
Her head is lifted, ears alert,
She hears each sound – heeds them all,
Calms each fear and soothes each hurt.

Thoughts which hover 'round all day –
And come so vividly at night
Vanish, with the cheerful ray
Of the nurse's little light.

In the silence shrills the phone,
She turns a bed down for another case;
Within she groans at work undone,
Yet greets him with a smiling face.

And so it goes night after night,
Sometimes better, sometimes worse,
But her presence makes things bright:
The reason folks love the night nurse.

Miriam Pulsifer, Class '52B

Undergraduate Students
February Class of '53

To the V.G., where classes go,
The student nurses, row by row,
To aid the sick of all their care
And relieve the pains that linger there.

There comes a class here, twice a year.
And to the V.G. we hold dear
The memories and friends we've made;
And in our minds they'll never fade.

Though the classes be large or small
They may be thin, stout, short or tall.
But of each class, its members show
Its unity and friendship glow.

To these students and many to come,
I say to them, "Oh, don't be dumb.
Enjoy your class, as you all see
Like we the class of '53."

Yvonne Myler, Class Feb. '53

An "If" for Grace Affiliates
(with the usual apologies to Rudyard Kipling)

If you can keep your head when all about you
The cold sterile water is running hot –
When you're supposed to wear a mask,
And of such a thing there just is not;
If you can to the Caseroom take a dinner,
And there they say "Oh, she's in the ward"
Well, if you can take this with a smile,
My girl, you deserve a gold award!

If you can feed three ounces to a baby,
And he does still refuse to burp,
Or over your clean nursery gown,
The whole formulae he does "slurp",
If you can change him every fifteen minutes,
And still wear a valiant grin
Then you're a fine nursery nurse,
My girl, you deserve to win!

If you can scrub for a delivery
And wait calmly for the Doctor to arrive,
And not contaminate a thing by waiting,
Waiting minutes ten, or five, or forty-five;
If you can stretch one single strand of stuture,
To do the work of three or four,
You're bound to win the Doctor's praises,
My girl, you needn't ask for more!

If you can balance two bed-pans,
To make a single trip instead of two,
And still close the door behind you;
(If no one bumps into you)
If you can cut five bouquets of flowers,
And change their water every morn' until they die,
And find room for them on one small dresser,
My girl, you're services we'll buy!

If you can get a cup of coffee in the morning,
　　Without the loss of arm or leg,
　And get your dishes to the table safely
　Without "scrambling" your hard-boiled egg;
If you can find a seat where none are vacant,
　　And still make room for just one more,
　　You'll not only enjoy your breakfast,
　　My girl, you'll make it to the door!

If you can make light of all of this nonsense
　　And look forward to a lot of fun,
　Then you'll love your Grace affiliation,
　My girl, the battle will be half won!

Aubrey Young, Sept. '54

Grace Affiliation

On September first, nineteen fifty four
We started out on a little tour
Of GMH – our very first day
There we were for a three-month stay.

To the Case Room first I was assigned
West wing next, and then to mind
The little babes in the Nursery
And give 'em plenty of T.L.C.

Oh joyous the mother in whose ears ring clear
The piercing cry of her baby dear;
She labored long, but 'twas not in vain
A babe has been born – to the world again.

God granteth the privilege to woman to bear
A child of her own, a baby dear.
Oh nurse, be gentle to her in travail,
Soon peace and happiness will prevail.

Oh nurse, take care of those little lives
For in their hands the future lies.
Oh mothers, be a guiding hand
And teach them always on truth to stand.

Oh babe asleep in your crib today,
Tomorrow an adult they will say;
To you I dedicate this verse –
For maybe you will be a nurse!

Cecilia Powell

H.C.H. Affiliation

At 6:30 sharp the wind did blow
We lucky six off to breakfast did go,
We ate it fast for we did find
that we had to in order to be there on time.

Our caps and scarfs we then put on
For the wind was cold it was barely dawn,
We rounded the corner holding on to our caps
With cold red noses that ran like taps.

Up University Avenue we trotted fast
Thinking "oh dear time has come at last
To begin another exciting day
In that red building across the way".

Cole and Cameron hurried along
To reach Gyro I at the ring of the gong,
They looked sharp dressed in their gowns and mask
Cheerfully doing whatever was asked.

Foote hurried along carrying her size ten shoes
Looking as though she had the blues,
Kerr, Lawson and Gordon coming along in the rear
Had D and V they could hardly bear.

The door flew open we six breezed in
With blood red hands and frozen chins
To the right of us as we rushed down the hall
Sat some students talking and having roll-call.

The tiny room at the end of the hall
Was full of affiliates all having a draw,
The smoke like a cloud blew out the door
And knocked the six of us flat to the floor.

At last time came for us to report to the floors
Where we saw children sleeping as we passed by the doors
The night report was read right away
So we started to work without delay.

We six shall never forget those twelve weeks
When we cared for the kids who were all so sweet,
Some of them cried both night and day
But we comforted them each in his own way.

Betty (unknown)

Famous Last Words of the Class of Sept. '55

Marion Gordon – "I'm through with men."
Dorothy Creelman – "No more blind dates for me!"
Cecilia Powell – "I must put up my hair tonight."
Lola Evans – "He's grounded."
Marilyn MacLean – "I'm going to clean my room tomorrow!"
Barb Lynds – "I'm Barb."
Pat Lynds – "I'm Pat."
Erna Geyer – "I'll put that in my diary."
Jennie Hanright – "I'm letting my hair grow!"
Norma Hughes – "Let's get mobile!"
Marilyn Moores – "Anyone want a date with a Newfoundlander?"
Helen Smith – "I'm on a DIET!"
Martha Harlow – "I hope I'm not nominated."
Barb Harvey – "Wake me!"
Betty Ann Ross – "Any brown envelopes?"
Anne Harvey – "I'll meet you at the elevator in five minutes!"
Carol Cole – "No more night duty for a while, I just came off."
Ariel Sanderson – "Zzzzzzzzzzzz."
T.S.O. – "Your class will be going into BLOCK."
12:00 MIDNIGHT – "We still have a few minutes."

Class Sept. '55

Songs of Our Times

 6:00 a.m. – "You'll Get Used to It"
 7:00 a.m. – "We're Here Because We're Here"
 8:00 a.m. – "Nobody Knows "Da Trouble I Seen"
 9:00 a.m. – "Traffic Jam"
10:00 a.m. – "Cool, Cool Water"
11:00 a.m. – "Smile Awhile"
12:00 p.m. – "Bread and Gravy"
 1:00 p.m. – "Give Me Five Minutes More"
 2:00 p.m. – "Where Are You Now That I Need You?"
 3:00 p.m. – "The Birth of the Blues"
 4:00 p.m. – "He's Dead But He Won't Lie Down"
 5:00 p.m. – "Who Threw the Overalls in Althea's Chowder?"
 6:00 p.m. – "The Last Mile Home"
 7:00 p.m. – "At Last"
 8:00 p.m. – "There'll Be a Hot Time in the Old Town Tonight!"
 9:00 p.m. – "Tea for Two"
10:00 p.m. – "Walking My Baby Back Home"
10:15 p.m. – "Dragnet"
11:00 p.m. – "Mr. Sandman"
12:00 p.m. – "Why Was I Born?"

Class Sept. '55

We'll Never Forget

Why Marion Gordon lost her ring.
The surgery performed on Marilyn's wrist. Who done it?
Our gripe about eating meals in 15 minutes –
and the "egg a day".
Betty Lawson's red plaid pyjamas.
The probie who told the doctor that there was
no "Mr. Kelly Pole" on the ward.
Getting fancy words out of the medical dictionary for the
morning report to impress the day staff.
Dot Creelman's first scrub a tatoo-ectomy.
Barb Lynds delivering a baby at the San.
Singing "Happy Birthday" into the phone to get ice cream
from the kitchen on Night Duty.

Class Sept. '55

Can You Imagine

Enough food in the 4th floor kitchen?
Saturday night without Fred Hearne?
Esther Rice with cigarettes?
Jeanette with long hair?
Never missing a phone call by "just five minutes"?
Training without Night Duty?
Miss McInnes getting undisturbed sleep?
Marilyn without dates?
Barb MacKay as a dumb brunette?
A Barn Dance in the Ballroom?
A swimming pool up on the sundeck?
Pay, for overtime duty?
The Grace without Lysol?
No last-minute cramming for exams?
A private phone in every room?
Starting as probies all over again?
The O.R. without Dr. Ballem?
Having Dr. Charman for a patient?

Class Sept. '55

Ode to "Our Class"

We came in September, the year '50
Some feeling glum and some feeling nifty.
With some from Cape Breton, and some from N.B.
While some left the country and some left the sea.
As we gazed at each other a feeling of dread
Came over us all for what lay ahead.
We all look so timid, so lost and forlorn,
Our eye still half open from that first early morn.
As we leafed through our textbooks and saw all the work,
We prayed that our hearts and our hands would not shirk.
There was Hygiene and Drugs and Solutions and such,
Would we ever be able to learn so much?
As the days passed to months, and the months to a year,
We finally realized our hearts belonged here.
For the friends we had made and for each thoughtful deed,
Had moulded us into a class that would lead.

Barbara Miller & Jean Harris, Class Sept. '55

To Us Seniors

We are now in the last lap – a real senior,
And, we feel older, wiser, more mature
We expect the others to hold the door,
And let us go first on an elevator.
From other students we want respect in every way.
But, nurse – did you deserve respect today?

Today, you were in charge on 7 West.
Did you organize the work – make things clear to the rest?
You helped the internes, and made rounds with doctors;
But did you turn any patients; prevent any bedsores?
Or were some things done – just any old way?
Nurse – did you deserve respect today?

Tomorrow you're senior on 4th floor, South –
But it won't hurt you to clean Mrs. Phair's mouth.
You'll give the pills – give them all the care.
Won't you take time to comb Granny Slaunwhite's hair?
If you want respect in every way,
Nurse – be sure you earn that respect each day.

Sure, you're busy with work to do at the desk –
But, you've time for answers when others ask.
You see an empty glass on Mr. Moore's table
Won't you pick it up – or aren't you able?
It's the things you do, and the things you say
That makes you deserve respect, each day.

Every bed may be full – no space for a chart;
But there's always room for a human heart.
Senior, wipe off your smugness – put your hands in the dirt.
A spot on your apron – has it ever hurt?
When you work with, and not over, the others, they'll pay
To you, the respect you deserve today.

After 7 p.m., you went out on a date.
Did you abide by rules – or come in late?
If, on wards you expect a bit more honour;
Don't have a "morning, after the night before".
It is then other students have a right to say, "Nay,
I cannot respect my Senior today".

Someday, the Head Nurse of Peace, Healing and Love
Will sign off our charts in the ward up above.
And, when His report is written for the Saints,
May His comment on our work be "No Complaints".
From now, until then, let us all work – and pray
That we will earn a little respect each day.

Myrtle Rogers, Class Sept. '55

Neurosurgery Night Duty

A patient said to me one night,
"Nurse, you must be tired," and I thought "You're right!"
But I said, "No, not really;" and put on a bright smile,
"Morning will be here, in a little while."

I sat on the desk, and started to think,
When a tiny voice said, "I want a drink."
If water cost money these folks would be broke!
Oh, God, thank you, thank you, little Tony spoke.

Down the hall came an ambulance case
An unconscious man, with not much left of his face.
Then, the endless rounds of turn, rub and check,
And sometimes I thought – He's only a wreck
Why keep him alive, when he's almost dead?
But, then, one night, he turned his head.
Oh, God, thank you, thank you, Mr. Brown turned his head.

A telephone call – a boy's coming down from Glace Bay,
His parents came with him, and they pray,
"Please, Father, please, make our Jimmy alright."
And I know, that we have to help God tonight.
They say to us, "He's our only son, Jim
And he is so good – why did it happen to him?"

I try to tell them we will do all we can
To make him better, for his one sister, Anne.
One night, a week later, he opens his eyes – but can he see?
"Jimmy, what am I?"
"You're a nurse – but where's my daddy?"
Oh, God, thank you, thank you, Jimmy can see.

Sure, I'm tired of feedings – there are so many to give.
But I am not tired of helping people to live.
And I'm sick of blood pressures, check pupils and pulse

But, when a patient walks home, I see the results.
Of the monotonous chores that I have done,
Perhaps I helped in the battle they've won,
So, I won't say "I'm tired." – I'll put on a bright smile,
And morning will be here in a little while.

Myrtle Rogers, Class Sept. '55

Us

Introducing the class of Feb. '55 –
Twenty in number are we.
We herewith enclose,
In a versicle prose,
Our brief, epic history.

'Twas the fateful day of Jan. 29
When off the deep end went we.
We woke up at six –
Felt like writing to Dix
And moaned to ourselves "woe is me".

To get our procedures according to Hoyle
Has long been our one ambition.
To do this we strove,
By Miss Nott we've been drove,
To gain for ourselves our admission.

The "care of the hair", a procedure we learned,
Miss Shepard us kindly related.
"Place a towel on the bed
And comb well the head –
Avoid being contaminated.

Take the pediculicide and soak well the head
With a piece of absorbent cotton.
With the 'cides enwrapped
In an O.R. cap,
In eight hours you'll have probably caught 'em."

To dispose of contents of bedpan and urinal,
Miss Robertson finds it safer –
To creep down the hall,
Clinging close to the wall
And put in incinerator.

And so we go on to sterile technique –
To needles, and post-operative care.
All hands to the fore,
We sleep in no more,
And advance on a wing and a prayer.

Eleanor Graham & Joan Gregson, Class Feb. '55

Days Spent in the Nurses Infirmary

From the experiences of training,
We must not forget
Those days in the Infirmary
Where nurses do fret,
And wait for the day
When a white sheet will be signed
By the doctor giving discharge –
Until the next time.

It may be just a cold
Or it may be D & V
Which we contracted at "the Children's"
While nursing the wee.
But I'll bet it's a week
In the Infirmary we stay
Think of the lectures we miss
And that deduction of pay!

In the Infirmary our daily care
Begins at nine
With the call for breakfast
And Mrs. Laver's chime.
Our temps are then taken
Then a rub with alcohol.
Gee! This place isn't really so bad after all.

Our beds are then straightened
And the treatment is begun
With pills and compresses –
From those needles I run.
Soon the doctor makes rounds
And we await for the news
Be it sad or be it glad
We have neither to choose.

And oh how those days drag
And seem so long
While the sun shines brightly
But in bed we belong.
We must take our medicine
And penicillin too.
I wonder if our patients,
Mind those needles like we do?

But soon comes evening
With the long awaited visiting time.
Our friends try to cheer us
And tell us we all look fine.
But if on isolation
At the door they must stop.
We wouldn't want them to contract
Hepatitis or chicken pox.

And then comes the day
When the white sheet is signed
By the doctor giving discharge.
Yes, we are back to the grind.
So on duty we do go
And a different attitude we take
By the experience we've just had.
Better nurses we hope to make.

Dot Creelman, Class '55B

What Nursing is to Me

Is nursing a profession to
Which glamour holds the key?
Or rather one of service?
That's what nursing is to me.

A pale, still face; a sudden smile,
Though weak, so good to see,
Brought by my humble comfort –
That's what nursing is to me.

To feel the satisfaction when
The child from pain is free,
Or relieve his heartfelt sobbing,
That's what nursing is to me.

The aching feet: the tired back,
What trifles these can be!
When with each task, a meaning,
That's what nursing is to me.

To comfort sick and helpless,
Needs no magic, old or new,
But the heart and hands God gave us,
What does nursing mean to *you*?

Betty Ann Ross, Class '55B

Motherly Advice

"Deer Ma, if you is able,
Please wire me a cable,
About the truth and facts of this here life,
I is really in a muddle,
On just when and where to cuddle,
To da man wats gon and asked me for his wife."

"Well dotter, quit yer frettin'
Cause you'll only find it gettin' you nowhere
but in an Irish Stew.
Just love him though he grieves yew,
Leaves yew, or deceives yew,
Cause men is men, dat's ma advice to yew.

They'll say that they adore yew,
When they actually abhor yew,
An REALLY luv yer money in da bank,
They'll honor and obey you,
Just to hurt yew and dismay yew,
'Till yew wish someone wud make yew walk the plank.

So dotter, Mama heed yew,
Be his comfort when he needs yew,
An please him lots by wearin silks an lace.
Cause there's no use jawin' 'bout them,
This ol' world wud be a pretty dreary place widout them."

Betty Ann Ross, Class '55B

Our Magic Work

You walk, your feet are sore;
You can't stand living anymore;
It's tragic.
The phone will ring, it's not for you;
It's raining out, you feel so blue;
It's tragic.
There was no mail today – at least, for you;
You wonder what this cruel, cold, world is coming to.

You're hungry, but the kitchen's bare;
You're tired, but must wash your hair;
It's tragic.
The alarm goes off, you sigh and groan
"Oh why oh why did I leave home!"
It's tragic.
You trudge on duty in a gloom,
And sigh and force a smile as you go in a room.

The patient smiles, (you still feel blue)
And then he says, "I'm glad it's you."
It's MAGIC.
Your gloom drifts off into the air,
And suddenly you seem to care.
It's MAGIC.
And as the day goes on, you find
To make others happy, it's worth going through.
And suddenly you know…
The MAGIC's in the work you do.

Betty Ann Ross, Class '55B

1st Day O.R.

You must be observant and efficient too.
Remember, a life may depend on you,
But how? We complained, can we be all this
Just look down below – oh joy, what bliss!
With everyone tense, and voices quite low
They're removing a bunion from somebody's toe.

2nd Day

Today you will scrub, our friends declared,
As we very proudly in green appeared,
At least – we entered the surgery room,
All ready to scrub – with mop and broom.

3rd Day

This morning we float, and eyes all agleam,
At last to be part of the surgical team,
The very first order was given to me,
Fetch a large airway quick as can be
From Dr. Ballem in Surgery E.
What's that? I puzzled, quite lost you see,
Then asked this question of Dr. B.,
And wonder of wonders, his mouth opened wide,
As he invited, "look down inside".

4th Day

At last to scrub, the time was here
And Dr. At--- stood quite near,
With bated breath and faces tense,
We passed to him the instruments,
Ne'er had a surgeon worked before
Without his trousers, I am sure,
For they had fallen to the floor.

5th Day

The end has come,
All I have done,
With those who say,
The OR's fun.

Rosemarie Masey, Class '56B

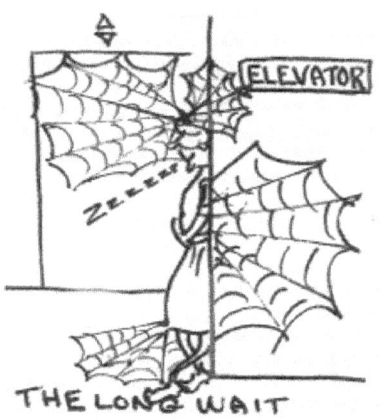

To the Students at the VGH

The nurses go
Between the beds row on row.
Care for the sick, and at T.S.O.[2]
Reports are read from nights ago
Scarce heard by doctors there below.

We are now graduates, short days ago
Were students, cleaned bedpans, saw urinals glow.
Buzzed and were buzzed
And still we work at the V.G.H.
Take up our duties, as you go
To you from tired hands we throw
The lamp, it's heavy, but hold it high
If you break faith with those who lie
We'll make you go, the nurses say
At the V.G.H.

Carole Reynolds, Class '58A

---

[2] Training School Office

40th Reunion VGH Class '61A – Barrington, June 2001

We are the chosen
By Marg to come here
To her house near the ocean
As summer draws near.

We've gathered together as we have
In the past
To renew our friendships
To just have a blast.

During three years of study, exams
And R.N.s
We started a friendship
40 years could not end.

We traveled, married, and had children
And then, we couldn't let go
Of the ties that had bound us
So long ago.

We had marvelous food, we did it ourselves
Had at our disposal a continuous lunch
We dined in Shelburne on Saturday night
And had fun drinking Florence Nightingale punch.

With food and the drinks to round out our cheeks
We'll all be loosening our waistbands for many weeks
We needed the beach walks, the laughter, the jokes,
The trip to the cape, the view of the boats.

We savoured the fun of yard sales and fairs,
Committed to memory what we beheld there
Of 60 year olds doing what we'd never tell,
Sitting on tilt-a-whirls and carousels.

So we'll leave this reunion with many emotions
Look to the future, put the next plans in motion
We will remember – we'll never forget
Class '61A – was the best class yet!

Pat Perry, Class '61A

45th Reunion '61A

The plan was set
5 years ago.
To P.E. Island
We would go.

It's forty-five years,
They've gone by so fast.
But friendships forged then
Were meant to last.

The business meeting over,
And then the fun began.
The jokes and wine were flowing
The feeling was quite grand.

Then Sally donned her uniform,
Around the room the smiles did grow,
The bib and apron, shoes and pins.
She certainly stole the show.

There were gifts and lots of scrapbooks,
And posters and more laughs,
There were memories shared among us,
With all the old photographs.

There were butterflies and gardens,
And lobster to be sure;
Anne of Green Gables,
And a double decker bus tour.

Just for a moment
Lorna and Pat became ill.
I think to remind us
We are nurses still.

Before our meetings were finished
We had one more chore,
To choose the site for our 50th,
You could tell we were ready for more!

Halifax was the place selected,
Suggestions were given, a tentative plan,
It really should be expected,
We chose the place where our class began.

But it really could not be over,
We said with tears and a sigh,
Then here we were talking and packing,
Already saying goodbye!

Pat Perry, Class '61A

A Question of Belief

Do you ever think of God
The same way that I do?
Do you ever think of God
With feelings deep and true?

Do you wonder how He made the world?
The earth, the skies, the seas?
Can you truly see these things unfurled
And still not praise His deeds?

Can you see the useless life we lead,
The days that pass as night –
Filled with hate and guilt and greed!
Surely these aren't right.

Do you know we're of His mould,
His image to be exact.
We've heard the story retold,
Fact upon fact, upon fact.

And yet we come just when in need
And only then, it's true;
It's then we give His love full heed
Kneeling in our pew.

Now can you go to church each week
With all your love to give?
Well if you can, my honored friend,
I'd give my all your life to live.

Gail Warren, Class '61B

A Tribute to '61B for 55th Reunion, August 2016

Springtime of life was on their side,
When first they came together.
From backgrounds various and wide,
Daughters and sons of carpenters,
Of doctors, farmers too;
It mattered not, for in their quest,
Together they all grew.

Those Springtime years they journeyed through
Both fair and stormy weather,
Time rushed on by; with much to do.
All too soon then, Summer came;
And in those busy days,
Immersed in work and family life,
They lived life in a haze.

But Springtime bonds would hold them fast,
As they strived to keep in touch.
Solid ties would far outlast
Great distances and diversity,
In ways they could not know;
That very bonding fed their souls,
And ever thus was so.

Then suddenly, upon them came
The Autumn season of their lives,
Still when together much the same,
Despite their outward looks.
Maturity was good;
Though some had passed on, as they all must,
Full knowing they too, would.

Wintertime finds them wondering
How did so much time go by?
And gently now the gifts they bring,

As they once more come together;
Compared to days long gone,
Is simple GRATITUDE and JOY,
For all that they have done.

Joyce (Stevens) Baxter, Class '61B

A Nurse's Prayer

Because the day that stretches out for me
Is full of busy hours, I come to Thee
To ask Thee, Lord, that thou wilt see me through
The many things that I may have to do
Help me to make my beds the smoothest way.
Help me to make more tempting every tray.
Help me to sense when pain must have relief.
Help me to deal with those borne down by grief.
Help me to take to every patient's room
The light of Life to brighten up the gloom.
Help me to bring to every soul in fear
The sure and steadfast thought that Thou are near.
And if today, or, if tonight, maybe,
Some patients in my care put out to see
To face the great adventure we call death,
Sustain them, Father, in their parting breath.
Help me to live throughout this live-long day
As one who loves Thee well, dear Lord, I pray;
And when the day is done, and evening stars
Shine through the dark above the sunset bars,
When weary quite, I turn to seek my rest,
Lord, may I truly know I've done my best.

Ruth Winant Wheeler

It all Began in '63

It all began in '63,
when wide-eyed and green we met at the tea
We invaded 6th floor for a 3-year spell
If these walls could talk, what tales they would tell
Of long gab sessions with laughter and fags
Endless backcombing and numerous gags
Rollers and piks and sunburns from hell
From a roast on the roof that didn't go well.

Of one loaf of bread for all of the floor
The kippers, the jello, and the scrubs and what's more
Trips thru the tunnel on the run and what for
To let someone in thru the auditorium door

Of trips to the Doria and the Gardenview
No wonder they called it the gag and spew
Amelia, Mrs. Whalen, the curfew violations
Lipstick and Poosie and other sensations.

We twisted and shouted to the Beatles and Stones
Relished our parties and learned our bones
Then finally the day that black band arrived
To our surprise and delight we had all survived.

Forty years have passed and here we are
Our knees and hips aren't quite up to par
Our minds and our memories are fading fast
But one thing for sure we can still have a blast.

Sue (Campbell) Carter
Marg (Grandy) Hibbert
Joanne (Dennison) McCormick
Jude (Shakespeare) Bell
Class '66A

Untitled Memories

In the month of January '63
A group of young probies came to sip tea,
And shyly met the gang that someday,
Would graduate as '66A.

We unloaded our bags on that famous 6th floor,
Was it really ready for what was in store?
Our neighbours would soon be our very close friends,
The lifeline on which three years would depend.

If the sixth floor walls could talk today
We can only imagine what they might say,
Of cross-legged powwows, sprawled in the halls,
The shrieks, the laughter, the pay-phone calls.

The borrowing of cigarettes, rolling hair,
Or groaning with sunburns from the roof upstairs.
Remember the elevators loaded for bear,
With starch and stripes and bouffant hair.

Remember the classroom with skeletons and beds,
Probie Block memories that stay in our heads.
If Miss Joncas could over the podium peep
She'd have seen at a glance, we were all asleep.
And you were really out cold, if you cannot recall
How she exited, talking, from classroom to hall.

Then in Jude's basement, blue band celebrations,
Some guys heard of this and made visitation.
These crashers we'd find would cause the demise
Of many of those steadys and hometown guys.

The Childrens', the N.S., the San and the Grace,
More study, more testing, all part of the race.
So much to learn and so many frights,
Like Miss Vincent, the O.R., and first senior nights.

Remember when enemas were mixed in a can,
By shaking old soap in the water you ran.
Remember the panic of one pill gone missing
And the lectures we had on the hazards of kissing.

Our social lives we rarely neglected
The big question was, would we be detected?
Sneaking through tunnels, or past the front desk
We gave Mrs. Whalen, and Amelia no rest.

Our favourite haunts were many and varied
Of parties and dancing we never were wearied.
Frat parties, ship parties to name but a few,
The Ladies Beverage Room made its debut.

Jude and Sue played tennis, but under pretense,
While cruising the interns who walked by the fence.
The Beatles appeared on Ed Sullivan's stage
The Victory Lounge and Captains Cabin all the rage.

So enjoy the reunion, have a talk with old friends,
Remember the times we had rounding life's bends,
Through good times and bad times, one factor's okay,
You can't take the spirit from '66A.

Susan (Campbell) Carter, Class '66A

A Glimpse Inside

It's not as though I've always thought
Of life and love and dreams well-sought,
For many days I've gazed this way
But not such serious games to play.
Castles and knights and princesses fair
Graced my moods when I wasn't there;
Or hide-and-seek or some childish game
Surrounded existence – no claim to fame.
'Twas then that dreams were based on beauty
To be "grown-up" was a little girls duty.
And then at dusk I'd slip between
Sheets of yellow and pink and green,
Half aware of the silent nearness
Of the gentle sandman and sleep's sweet dearness.
My world existed of laughter and tears
Not unlike my future years.
But now I see how life can be.
At times so beautiful and free.
At other times a dingy gray
Hangs over me and clouds my day.
A day of cares and strife and tears
Bringing to light my hidden fears
That all the thoughts composing me
Are wrong, so biased, not to be.
Then I aspire to greater heights
Of love and joy and careless plights
Of happiness and warmth in being
Not scarred by hate or lack of seeing.
But now I hold my future in my hands
To shape and mould my present plans
Concerning me and those so near
That my own dreams they will hold dear
The "future" is a misty word
Encompassing an unknown world.
To open like a dewy rose

To live, to breathe and then to close.
I oft times yet sit and dream
Of things quite like my childhood scheme
Of perfect days and perfect nights
Shielded by dreamland's lights.
And then reality creeps in
Not harsh, but soft to glow within
My senses, stirred by my desire
To alleviate suffering and gain much higher
Goals than wealth and riches great
As in my childish dreams of fate.
For now I know the wealth of smiles
And tender moods to warm the wiles
Of the unknown, untrodden trail.
You look to me to soothe your pain
And I will try, and yet again
I ponder and think of my own care
You look to me 'cause I am there
And then "my" cares take wings and fly
'Cause you are there and I must try
To give of all that I can give
To help this day
Someone to live.

Marjorie Pringle, Class '72A

Nurse of the Future

Bloody messes scare me, surgery's not that neat,
I can't stand dressing changes, I gag at smelly feet,
Needles give me goose bumps, pruritus makes me itch,
I walk into I.V. poles and I'd faint at one small stitch,

My T.P.R.'s are wild, my charting is the pits,
I choke and just freeze helpless when someone's in a sitz,
Bedsores turn my stomach, enemas make me sick,
Bedpans make me vomit, asepsis just doesn't click.

My skills sometimes seem hopeless though I try and try again
But I do love all my patients – for them the strength I'll gain
To fight these nagging fears, I'm sure there must be worse…
Someday my dear instructor – I know I'll make a nurse!

Kim Ward, Class '80

Of Your Color or Race You Have No Choice

Of your color or race
You had no choice,
In selecting your father and mother
No voice,
But the road you take,
As you go along
The choices you make
Between right and wrong,
The words you speak and the deeds you do,
Are decided by nobody else, but YOU.

To the class of 1981, may your actions and deeds
Speak louder than words.

Class '81

It's Up to You

It isn't a question of what you've done
But what you intend to do,
For records past can't always last
And they'll not carry you through.

You may have won attention
That has travelled far and wide;
But unless you try for a goal more high
You'll be on the losing side.

For the race of life is keen today,
Competition reigns supreme.
We must be at our best to meet the test;
It's a case of going up stream.

Don't stop when you reach a certain point;
There are greater things to be done.
Unless you surpass, the rest will outclass
The work you've only begun.

Resolve and try to improve yourself,
Replace old laurels with new.
It isn't a question of what you've done,
But what you intend to do.

Lloyd Ira Miller

Leavin' the Old An' Greetin' the New

It's kinda tough t' hafta leave
So many folks you've learned t' know,
An' have 'em grip you and an' tell
How much they hate t' see you go!
It's kinda tough t' say goodbye
T' friends you've seen day after day –
It's hard t' break the happy bonds
O' comradeship, an' move away.

It's hard t' pack up all yer things
An' leave a cozy home behind –
The place where joys have come t' you.
Where neighbors all have been so kind.
An' when, at last, yer dearest pal
Is tryin' hard t' make a bluff
At bein' brave, an' breaks right down,
It's kinda tough – it's kinds tough!

But say! It's great t' find new friends
Just waitin' fer a chance t' show
How glad they are t' have you come
An' live with 'em! It's great t' know
That folks 're jus' about the same
No matter where you chance t' roam,
An' if you let 'em have their way
You'll soon be a feelin' right at home.

So it's a long farewell, old friends;
May God be mighty good t' you!
Across the miles an' down the years
You'll find my friendship always true.
An' now I turn with eager heart
T' meet whatever life extends –
T' greet the folks that welcome me,
An' try to make 'em all my friends!

Lawrence Hawthorne

Let's Keep in Touch

Just to keep in touch with someone,
And to understand their need,
Just to share with them your friendship,
Is a privilege indeed.

For life is so much brighter when your
Joys and cares you share,
And burdens seem much lighter when
A friend of yours is there.

There's nothing quite so precious on
This earth, it seems to me,
As the loyal friends who are so loyal,
Who understand so perfectly.

The little deeds of love are the things
That give a lift
And a friend who's true, who understands,
is surely God's own gift.

A smile, a word of kindness are the
Things that means so much…
So take the time to be a friend,
And please, let's keep in touch.

Virginia Swan

Graduation Night

Thank you for letting me
Have you as a friend.
Secrets never spoken
And the laughter and the tears.
It's graduation night, everything's all right
But it's time to say good-bye.

Memories come back to me
As my thoughts go back in time.
To parties and introductions
And getting to class on time.
Those excuses made for each other
Well, now the last one's mine.
It's graduation night, everything's all right
But it's time to say good-bye.

A special thanks to you,
I have to pass their way
Through their teaching and their caring
They've prepared us for this day.
They see, it's our time to go
And face the world, to make it on our own.
Good luck to everyone
And it's time to say good-bye.

Della May Scott, Class '47

Ode to VGH Nurses Alumni
1920-2020

We gather now to celebrate
Those men and women of our past,
Whose pride in what they did, so strong!
Whose words in Constitution say:
"Preserving history – a must".
Whose vision brings us to this day!

Go back in time one hundred years,
Imagine if you can, that world:
A shattered city on the mend;
A war to end all wars had passed,
The roaring 20's just begun,
Hope high, for peace at last.

The age of flight in infancy,
No CPR, and no TV,
No penicillin for a cure.
They did the best that they knew how,
To ease a pain, to dress a wound,
To soothe a fevered brow.

Then came the Great Depression years,
Unbidden as the prairie winds,
That blew the earth from farm and field,
And stole away the fertile soil.
The impact felt from Coast to Coast,
Made heavier their toil.

Soon, from afar dark shadows loomed.
The horrors of a Second War!
So many went when duty called,
Enduring much of pain and strife.
So many sacrificed their all,
And bravely gave their life.

Go back in time now fifty years,
Imagine if you can, that world:
Despite the changes all around,
Alumni carried on still true,
To work begun, those years long past.
Enrolment numbers grew.

Our youthful learning filled a need;
Saw life and death unlike our peers.
We shared as soldiers do in war,
Made bonds, that would become the guide,
To meet with purpose, comrades ALL;
Wearing a sense of pride.

The faces change, as time does too.
By-laws revised to meet the needs.
A Constitution keeps us strong,
Support for learning, still is key.
Rich Artifacts that tell a tale,
Our Archives FULL – of history.

We gather now to celebrate!
And tho' the future yet unclear,
These contributions of the past,
Displayed with pride, for all to see,
So generations yet to come,
Will know our legacy,

Joyce (Stevens) Baxter, Class '61B

Written to the Music of Popular Tunes

To the Tune of: "Land of Hope & Glory"
Probie Song, Class '53A

We are the probies of '50
Here with aims so high
Wishing to leave behind us
Names that will not die
Though we may be tired,
Discouraged for a while
We try to answer each call
With a smile.

Class '53A

To the Tune of: "The Glow Worm"
Probie Song, Class Sept. '56

We are the probies of the V.G.
All you seniors please go easy.
We do our best from wards to classes,
Cleaning bed-pans, and washing glasses.
There's a buzzer, better answer,
Here's a bedpan, sit right there, sir!
Thus it goes from day to day,
We've no time for play!

We practice out on Mrs. Chase,
She is very hard to place,
One leg goes up and the other down
How that makes Miss Rundle frown!
She fills us with many a fact
On how to rub a patient's back,
Our cerebrums grow so dim –
We can't think of him.

In three short years we will finish,
Then you'll see those stripes diminish,
First our cap, and then in white
We will be on the final night.
But – there's lots more work cause we've just started,
From our past life we've just parted,
Yet we're proud of the life we've picked,
The class of '56

Class '56

To the Tune of: "Roll Out the Barrel"
Probie Song, Class '61B

We are the probies
We have a barrel of fun
We are the probies
We've got the blues on the run,
We don't know nothing
We're wet behind the ears,
But you know ignorance is bliss
So give us three years.

We're young, we're green
We don't know where we're going
We made some foolish blunders
But we're learning, and we're growing,
We'll make it, we can make it
We'll get our caps someday,
Until that date we'll celebrate
And altogether say

(Chorus)

Class '61B

To the Tune of: "Mem'ries"
50th Reunion '61B, 2011

Of how much we had to learn,
Of how difficult it all was.
And the way we were.

Scattered pictures;
Some of laughter, some of tears
Of the time we spent together
Talking late at night.

Can it be that it was all so long ago
And that now we find us gathered here.
If we had the chance to do it all again,
Tell me, would we, could we?

Mem'ries, mitered corners, bed baths all,
High up soap suds, h.s. lunches,
And the smell of alcohol.

So it's the laughter, we will remember,
Whenever we remember, the way we were,

THE WAY WE WERE.

Joyce (Stevens) Baxter, Class '61B

Written by Authors Unknown

The Bedpan

*With apologies to American author Joyce Kilmar
and his lovely poem "Trees"*

I think that I shall never scan,
A poem lovely as the pan;
When brought to me with urgent speed,
To satisfy that pressing need.

That pan that does in chill of autumn,
Feel nice and warm against the bottom.
Mayhap, it may, in winter wear
A fur trimmed edge – but I don't care.

For on its contours I have lain
To quell that supra-pubic pain.
Poems are made by foolish man,
But only nurses bring the pan.

Ode to a Johnny Shirt

No dressy lines distinguish you from others,
I can't imagine why you were designed,
But there you hang – 'twixt neck and knees suspended
With ties behind.

Far, far too short to cover where most needed –
Often your ties are missing from the rear
When icy breezes chill posterior regions
I clutch you near.

Perhaps with health's returning I'll don you,
And when my friends come in some sunny day –
Forgetting you I'll quickly rise to greet them as
They faint away.

But if my days in this world are numbered
And if they toll for me the parting bell –
St. Peter will take one look at my quaint raiment
And say "Oh W-e-l-l".

The Nurses Cap

It is more than a cap that they place on her head,
It's the symbol of comfort and joy she will spread.
It's the rededication of heart, mind and hand,
To the work she has chosen, the life she has planned.
It's a goal she worked hard for, a moment so dear.
It's a milestone indeed in her noble career.

Nurse Defined

A nurse is a marvelous compound of science and nature.
She is trained like a doctor,
Registered like a Holstein cow,
Starched like a full dress-shirt,
And salaried like a farm hand.

But can she do miracles!
She can make a five foot sheet cover a six foot bed,
And shake down a clinical thermometer
Without dislocating her wrist
Or putting out her patient's eye.

God Made a Nurse

God made a Nurse,
He made her heart, brave, true and kind,
And like the mountain streams, her mind,
As crystal clear, yet swift and deep
As where its waters, rush and sweep.

He made her hands strong, tender, skilled
Their touch with His own pity filled,
And gave to make His nurse complete
A sense of humour wholesome, sweet,
God made a nurse – Thank God.

A Nurse's Prayer of Compassion

Lord help me
To bring comfort where there is pain
Courage where there is fear
Hope where there is despair
Acceptance when the end is near
A touch gentle with
Tenderness, Patience
And Love.

Nurse's Prayer

Oh My God, teach me to receive the sick in your Name.
Give to my efforts success for the glory of your Holy Name.
It is your work, without you, I cannot succeed.
Grant that the sick you have placed in my care be abundantly blessed, and not one of them lost because of any neglect on my part.
Help me to overcome every temporal weakness,
And strengthen in me whatever may enable me
To bring joy to the lives of those I serve.
Give me Grace, for the sake of your sick ones and those lives that will be influenced by them.
Amen

A Nurse's Prayer

No fame I crave,
Before my eyes
A simple goal I seek
I hope, just once before I die
To get sufficient sleep.

Just a Nurse

Gee, it's fun to be a nurse,
Means a lot of work, that's true,
But it has its funny moments,
Any nurse will say that too.

When we enter as a probie,
Dusting seems to be our lot,
And our hearts are filled with envy
Caps and bibs as yet we've not.

Soon we are the eager freshies,
Caps and bibs are spick and span,
And we try to do our duty,
Helping out where e're we can.

Now we are the busy juniors,
Cares and tasks fill all our day,
Bearing all the harder duties
And yet it leaves our spirits gay.

Here's our hope, O lofty seniors,
That our footsteps follow you –
But we know you hate to leave us –
Though your time with us is through.

Ten Commandments for Probies

Thou shalt obey thy seniors.
Thou shalt not bow down to orderlies
mistaking them for doctors.
Thou shalt not take the name of the T.S.O. in vain.
Remember the Sabbath Day to keep it holy.
Six days shalt thou labour and on the seventh day
shalt thou do all thy cleaning.
Honour thy seniors that thy days may be peaceful on the ward
to which T.S.O. has assigned thee.
Thou shalt not feel like murder
when thou cometh from duty at 9 p.m.
Thou shalt not ruin thy feather cut with a hair net.
Thou shalt have no time to thyself for any pleasure.
Thou shalt not feel aggravated at false witness against thyself.
Thou shalt not grumble at thy hard lot, at thy early rising,
at thy misery inflicting shoes, at thy probie uniform, at thy
demonstration practices, at thy classes on p.m.s., at thy aching
feet, at thy tired back, nor at any other thing
that comes in the life of a probationer.

A Show to Remind Us

"The Snake Pit" – The case room.
"Joan of Arc" – Johnnie.
"For Whom The Bell Tolls" – At 6 a.m.
"All This And Heaven Too" – Training.
"Chicken Every Sunday" – Whatta dream.
"The Egg and I" – Affiliation breakfast.
"So Proudly We Hail" – Our training school.
"The Best Years Of Our Lives" – these???
"Dark Passage" – The tunnel.
"A Little Bit Of Heaven" – Vacation.
"I Remember Mamma" – Don't we all.
"Major and The Minor" – At the Grace.
"Two Years Before The Mast" – The Intermediates.
"How Green Was My Valley" – Before affiliation.

Thoughts of a Graduate

At last the day has dawned,
That day my dreams looked to;
My heart still holds a song
At sunrise's golden hue.

I'll think of days behind,
At V.G.H. they sped,
Yet still thoughts will bind
Them to the days ahead.

I'll think of them sometime
When all alone I'll be,
And thro' the years be mine
The dreams, which now I see.

Operating Room Psalm

Mr. Carruthers is my head nurse. I shall want no other.
He maketh me to scrub for hard surgeons.
He leadeth me into the operating room.
He restoreth my confusion.
He leadeth me through a mental labyrinth of cat-gut and cautery for technique's sake.
Yea, tho I go through the ordeals of a scrub nurse I fear no mistakes,
For my alphabet of sutures and sponges is with me.
It's precepts and directions comfort me.
A fable has been prepared for me in the midst of my experience.
My first operation has anointed my head with success and my spirit bubbleth over.
But darkness and shame shall follow me all the days of my life.
I have lost the specimen and I shall dwell in disgrace forever.

Class Prophecy 1939

Approximately three years ago tonight this graduating class
Made up a group of probies who were quite
determined to pass
Their preliminary examinations so that sometime maybe they
Could take their place as graduates as they now do today.
Of course they had their ups and downs and days
when they felt blue
And even wished Florence Nightingale
could be told a thing or two
For starting such a training that so tried
ones powers of endurance
And you wrote your folks of things kept on,
they would be collecting
Your insurance, but each one to herself had said.
And each one
Felt she knew if others before her had to do
the same then surely she could too.

So now tonight that probie class feel very much elated
And find it hard to realize they have finally graduated.
Now that training days are o'er, they eager faces shout
What has the future got in store,
is what they would like to know
So fellow classmates here tonight your future I will state
Let's see what strange and startling thing
each one's future will take!

Marriages, marriages, marriages. The stats quite plain reveal
For almost every one of you will at the altar kneel
And take your vows and say I do
for better or for worse and show
The men that they were wise to have their wife a nurse.

Because even tho' brunette or blond and with seemingly
helpless look along with all her feminine charm
she is a marvelous cook.

When hubby takes a cold in the head
no doctor is called to improve him
To hurry quick her husband is sick
she just does something for him.

Just to summarize these 27 nurses we'll put to rhyme their
future sublime in just so many verses:

Miss Weir and Miss Brenhan might add Miss Lohnes too
entered into matrimony shortly after they were through so
their futures are quite definite to lead happy married lives and
this all three are going to do as all three
are perfect model wives.

Miss Whiston I sense and Cameron also Jean Neish and
Evelyn Potter will get their share of proposals but they just
don't think they ought'er, they just can't see it's worth it so
they will continue with their nursing.

Miss Cleveland will in future be a naval officer's 'bride', will
travel with her husband and in different parts reside, although
her friends at first will tell her never marry a sailor is their
advice; Miss Cleveland notwithstanding finds it
nautical and nice.

Miss Scott will marry the English Chap of that there's not a
doubt and go to Merry Olde England that she has heard so
much about, have a camouflaged cottage with sandbags round
the door. She'll be very happy even tho' there is a war.

Miss Fraser and Miss Douglas are really going places that
they both will marry two handsome flying aces who will
return from overseas and bring such honors for them and their
trophies at their feet because they both adore them.

Miss Smiley when a student nurse I've often heard her say
would like to nurse away up north and she would too
someday. But the well laid plans are nice and were as Bobby
Burns would say to oft go stray as is the way that Smiley's

plans turn out. For days in southern Africa Smiley will be pleased to stay as she would marry that Engineer who made her plans his way.

Then there are those in time of war will do nursing overseas. Miss Smith, Thompson, Hills, and Brown are just a few of these. The several others to enlist are Fletcher, Smart, and Rose and just what happened to these girls; well the story goes Miss Fletcher was the only one who came back to tell the tale. She said she waited for the rest but they refused to sail as all the nurses who were over there, and many of those who were sick, the opportunity was so good.
They all just took their pick.

Wilson, Sabine, and MacMichael will find their fortune in the west and will settle down and marry as so did all the rest.

Mr. Peters in the future will continue his vocation and also loving Nellie wherever his location.

Mr. Clark as we predicted will soon change his profession to composing symphonies and such which will in rapid succession bring wide acclaim and his name will among the famous be. And in Carnigie Hall the applause will fall on the Max Clark symphony.

And last but certainly not least, I am quite at a loss to tell you definitely what will happen to Mr. Ross. With that old guy independence that we know in days of yore and his great love of adventure, Mr. Ross will go to war. He there will win distinction and receive the Victoria Cross for his reasonable feats of bravery, such a man is Mr. Ross, he will travel to the Highlands, he will travel to the low and will join the foreign Legion; more than that I do not know.

In concluding fellow classmates there is something I would say. I hope I have not offended anyone in anyway as the future I have predicted are just sheer imaginations and I wish you all the best of luck in this your Graduation.

Life's Changed, Ain't It!

Came in trainin'
Years ago (seems like anyway)
Lots o' clothes
Lots o' money
Life's changed
Ain't it!

Now –
Up with the sun
Work all day
Come off duty
Look around –
Clothes all dirty
Tired out!

Stockings run
Caps withered
Cheques ain't in
Exams comin'
No white polish
I'm sick!

Friends gone out –
Sweater missin'
Nothin' to et
Off to bed
What, no toothpaste!
Borrow some!

Night duty
Classes every day
No mail
No ink to write
No stamps
And then my pen's gone!

Woes and misery
Work and failure
My gosh, we're almost thro'
How we'll miss it!
But Life's changed –
Ain't it?

To My Mother/To My Father

Mom…

The stretch of the years is now long past
Since I was your baby girl,
The years when you mended a broke doll
Or smoothed down a straying curl.

I've come since then to a woman's place
To my graduation day.
I'm a nurse – and the dream of my childhood hours
Stands achieved – and my heart is gay.

But mother, I know I could never have won
If your love hadn't helped me along.
I who was always so weak on the way
You who were ever so strong.

Your love and your help, and your kindly praise
These followed me through the years.
A million thanks well up from my heart,
God bless you – your joy and your tears.

You are my model – you are my ideal
Yours – ever the love that was true.
God couldn't be with me all of the time
So he gave me a mother like you.

And mother, if ever around my neck
The arms of a baby twine
I only ask God to be like unto you,
You – little mother of mine.

Dad…

Today I'm a nurse – it seems but a dream
I can hardly believe it's true.

My training is done – I have come to the end
And my first thankful thought is, of you.

You, my father, who helped me so much on the way
You whose love and whose faith was so strong…
Yours the kindness, the courage, the praise that was there
In times when the way seemed so long.

I know that you're proud, Dad, today as you see
Your nurse – just so late your wee tot,
But my pride in you, Dad, rings as strong in my heart
God love you – and bless you a lot.

This is only a verse – just a "thank-you" in rhyme
But its accents are happy and glad.
For it tells of the love that in gratitude comes
From a graduate nurse to her Dad.

And a Song to Make a Laugh

"Didy Boogie" – Gyro
"Bloop Bleep" – I/V
"Now Is The Hour" – 6 a.m.
"Lost Cord" – G.M.H.
"The Stars Will Remember" – And so will we.
"Down By The Old Mill Stream" – Old Wd. 16.
"Old Black Joe" – Well, Joe anyway.
"I Guess I'll Have To Change My Plans" – O.R. call.
"I Can't Get Started" – Early in the morning.
"I Don't Stand A Ghost Of A Chance" – Exam time.
"One O'Clock Jump" – The dance we always miss.
"Now The Day Is Over" – 7 p.m.
"Less Than The Dust" – Probies.

Question in Anatomy

What happens to the lap when one stands up?
Retires to the rear and pops up under an assumed name.

Motto for X-Ray

Let your light so shine through men that you may see their bad works and eliminate them.

My Roommate

What nightmare do I see at dawn
When I'm awakened by the gong?
My roommate!

Who takes up all my closet space
And trots around in my best lace?
My roommate!

Who chatters wildly in her sleep
And scares me so – I want to weep?
My roommate!

Who thinks soap operas are supreme
While I sit there and want to scream?
My roommate!

Who wants to sleep when I want to talk
And develops sore feet when I want to walk?
My roommate!

Who gets the patients giving presents supreme
While I get ones who only scream?
My roommate!

Who shares my sorrows and joys so few
Without whom, I could not do?
My roommate!

Needles

When one is ill and in one's bed
Without a care to be alive or dead
The nicest thing one can see is a nurse –
Approaching calling in a voice of glee
      NEEDLE!

She feels your arm, your buttocks broad
And with a thumb will gently prod –
To find a spot so firmly packed
You think "O Lord, I'm really wacked
      With that darn
      NEEDLE!"

She jabs and then she jabs again
"Don't move", she yells, "you'll feel no pain"
"Oh No? You're only half insane
      With the XO*X&%
      NEEDLE!"

Now that the ordeal is o'er
Now Ah! Ha! You know the score
There is no doubt whether punch or bore
      With that accursed
      NEEDLE!

And when at home you safely sit
By radio – you're smoke well lit
The wife says gently – giving you a fit –
      "Dear, please pass the –
      NEEDLE!"

A Nurse Has Feelings Too

Have you ever wondered how we feel
When we do the things we do?
Have you ever stopped to realize
That a nurse has feelings too?

Perhaps the smile upon her face
Is trying to hide her sorrows
Or the heart that's light and gay all day
Will be broke before tomorrow.

A nurse awaits the minute
That a newborn takes its breath
She calmly closes the glassy eyes
That have entered the sleep of death.

She wipes away the stubborn tear
That trickles down the cheek
And this could happen every day
Of every single week!

In emergencies she buries her face
And quietly buries her load
For that is but a narrow strip
Of life's wide weary road.

She sees the wasting away of time
By accidents, sickness and fear
And often has to bite her tongue
To resist a silent tear.

She shares the hurt of the little ones
Who in the long night weep
And pats the tiny curly heads
Till they drift back to sleep.

So if you think our hearts are cold
That's just the outer shell
For if our hearts could only talk
They'd have a lot to tell!

Today…Tomorrow…Always

We all have special treasures
That in memory transcend…
One of the very dearest
Is an old and cherished friend.

A friend is there when needed
Without pretense or ado.
Today…tomorrow…always,
His smile encourages you.

New friends we surely welcome,
Yet the ones who mean so much
Are endeared by fond memories
Of friendship's velvet touch.

A word of understanding,
An extended hand in need,
Remembrance of a token
Or a sweet and thoughtful deed.

What greater compensation
Or happiness can one find,
Than a friend in consonance
With your feelings, heart and mind.

Who may even disagree,
Yet will always understand;
Who greets you with a warm smile
And a friendly outstretched hand.

Acquaintances come and go
Like all fair-weather friends,
But those remaining faithful
Are unmoved by fads or trends.

In adversities of life,
When our hearts are sad and blue,
Today…tomorrow…always,
True friends come smiling through!

In thinking of our friendship,
Fond memories merge and blend.
I realize how fortunate
I am that you are my friend!

As I recount the friendships
That have lasted and are true,
Today…tomorrow…always…
I'm very grateful for you.

Thoughts at 3 a.m.

When the wards are dark and quiet
And the night is cool and still.
And the neurotic patients
Have stopped yelling for a pill.
When the shaded lights are burning,
By the desk and down the hall,
And the chirping of a cricket
Is the only sound at all,
That's when you get to thinking
And you see the strangest things
Your imagination brings.
I can picture the Crimea
And the Lady with the Lamp,
As she valiantly trudges
On inspection 'round the camp.
She held a candle in her hand
And I wonder did she know
How the feeble flame she kindled
Was to multiply and grow.
It brightened then a small confine –
Who was there to foresee
That later by a hundred years
The gleam would fall on me!
Who'ere is touched is set apart
To guard a sacred trust
To hold the light for others
To be honorable and just,
So tonight I sit and wonder
If my life will ever be
A magnifying of that flame
That came from her to me.
Will I build it up and pass it on
To ever brighter grow

Or will my influence cheapen it,
Cause it to flicker low.
May I ever do my very best
In making others see
What I can feel within my heart,
What nursing means to me.

Graduation Teardrops

Hello my dear friend, why the teardrops you say.
Well it's hard to explain in any one way.
You see, old comrade, graduation is here.
It signals the end of our last V.G. student year.

One teardrop for sadness, the next one for joy
And yet still another for the first special boy.
The door to a new life shall open today,
So many close buddies will soon move away.

Left behind are the books and the instructors we knew,
That helped us so much each year as we grew.
Two years, gossip and late worksheets we shared,
Showing some special way each of us cared.

Now, dear friend, do you see why I cry?
A beautiful part of life has gone by.
I hope you'll remember in all years to come,
Precious days that combined to make this special one.

Graduation Song

Only one song so much to say this is our Graduation Day. We made it through. Thank God I had someone there who understood me when I was blue. I'm going to miss you. Remember all the times we shared and all those who cared and all those memories will always stay with me.

I'd like to thank-you Mom and Dad for standing by me the whole way through; I'm so proud of you. And I hope you understand you'll never lose me, I still need you. I remember all those times I was packing up to leave and then I'd call you on the phone and you were always there for me.

To you who gave that little extra praise to help us make it through those days, we thank you, for understanding those times when we just didn't get it right. You said it was O.K. But now we're out on our own and I know we'll do alright. Just remember to share throughout your lifetime.

Written by Patients and Others

The Nurse

The world grows better year by year
Because some nurse in her little sphere
Puts on her apron and grins and sings
And keeps on doing the same old things.

Taking temperatures, giving the pills
To remedy mankind's numerous ills
Feeding the baby, answering the bells,
Being polite with a heart that rebels.

Longing for home and all the while
Wearing the same old professional smile,
Blessing the newborn baby's first breath,
Closing the eyes that are still in death.

Taking the blame for the doctor's mistakes
Oh, dear, what a lot of patience it takes –
Going off duty at seven o'clock,
Tired, discouraged and ready to drop.

But called back on special seven-fifteen,
With woe in her heart but it must not be seen,
Morning and evening, noon and night,
Just doing it over and hoping its right.

When we lay down our caps and cross the Bar,
Oh Lord, will you give us just one little star
To wear in our crowns, with our uniform new,
In that city above, where the head nurse is You.

Myrtle K. Wentzell, Patient at VGH, 1940

Kindness Heals

While convalescing in the hospital
Recovering from disease,
My nerves were often edgy
But were quickly put to ease
By the kindness of the nurses.
As they gave me constant care,
I could call them any hour,
In a jiffy they were there.
Oftimes I was discouraged,
In the dumps and feeling low,
Somehow the nurse's presence
Made all depression go.
May God bless all the nurses,
'Twas He who gave them skill,
A gift of understanding,
Patience, kindness and goodwill.

James E. McManus, Patient on 4th Floor

Tribute to the Night Nurse

She keep her lonely vigil through the dark and dreary night,
Alert and silent watching, in the shaded candlelight.
Her presence is a blessing, for she's ready to perform
The little tasks that make the patient comfortable and warm.
Kind, sensible and capable, and quiet as a mouse;
She brings a sense of peace and comfort to the troubled soul.
For we can go to bed and sleep and know that she is there
To watch o'er us with her wise and tender care.
God be with these good women as they watch the long night through,
And may they be rewarded for the splendid work they do.

Unnamed ex-patient

Oh, Florence Be Glad That You're Dead

There are many changes in nursing
Since the Nightingale oath we all read
They've taken the care out of nursing
Oh, Florence be glad that you're dead.

The lamp is no longer our beacon
We're using the intercom instead
To which nurses respond from an office
And need never go near the bed.

We no longer use the term patient
We call them clients instead
And decide their fate at a conference
By a team that never goes near the bed.

We've conquered the TB bacillus
And spirochetes we no longer dread
We have eradicated smallpox
Now an AIDS epidemic looms ahead.

We are back doing primary nursing
To improve our expertise, it is said
But most of our work is on paper
The nurse seldom goes near the bed.

We have upgraded our CPR knowledge
And brought patients back from the dead
To live the rest of their lives in limbo
With anoxic brains in their heads.

We have high tech scans and computers
With printouts that are easily read
Machines now monitor our patients
The nurse needn't go near the bed.

Hospitals are run as corporations
To keep finances out of the red
'Tis the budget that's all important
Not the patient who's lying in bed.

Your bedside care was the greatest
According to books that we're read
Today's nurse has forsaken her patient
Oh, Florence be glad you're dead.

Bunny Lord, St. Boniface

Playing Patient

I'm going to play patient for nurses in session
And tell them my views on their noble profession.
I know a few things I shall certainly mention
From sunrise to bedtime I've had their attention,
I've watched them come in with a smile meant to wheedle
Knowing well I was due to be jabbed with a needle.

I've been ill but I'll vow that I've seldom been surly
I've smiled when they brought my breakfast too early.
I've been awakened from sleep without any excuses
To swallow their pills and their daily fruit juices,
I've mouthed their thermometers many a minute
While they made my bed with me still lying in it.

I've ridden their wheelchairs, in blankets well swaddled,
Arm in arm with my nurse down the hallway I've toddled.
I've said not a word when their writing chore started.
I knew for the doctors my case must be charted.
I'd shout from the house tops and from every church steeple;
The nurses, God bless them, they are wonderful people.

Edgar A. Guest

The Nurse

That cap the nurse on duty wears
Is costlier than the bonnets gay
Worn by the wives of millionaires
Regardless of the price they pay.
'Tis something she herself can make,
A bit of linen, trimmed and turned
The right to it (for mercy's sake)
Was with three years of training earned.

That uniform of spotless white
Was costlier than a lady's gown,
'Twas bought with care by day and night
For those with illness stricken down.
The royal robes show royal birth
But every nurse's simple pin
Is emblematic of her worth;
A symbol she has toiled to win.

Oh gracious spirit, love imbued,
That can such tender care accord,
Perhaps it is, that gratitude
Must always be your best reward.
Now out of gratitude appears
This tribute, done in simple verse
Unto the dedicated years
Of all who chose to be a nurse.

Edgar A. Guest

Farewell

The day has come, the hour near
When we must leave her door
And take our separate pathways
In the world she trained us for
We never shall forget her and
Forever will decree our loyalty and praises
There is only one V.G.

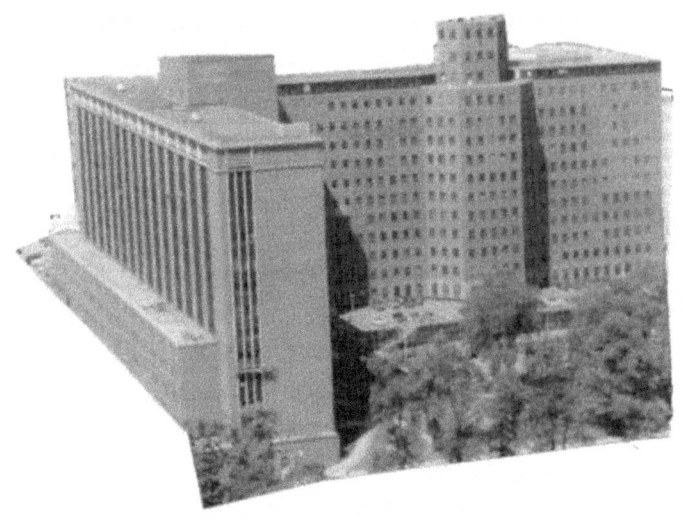

*VG Hospital and Centennial Building
(Photo: John Ashcroft)*

www.ingramcontent.com/pod-product-compliance
Lightning Source LLC
Chambersburg PA
CBHW071134090426

42736CB00012B/2123